Polygons in Our World

Reason with Shapes and Their Attributes

Brian Armstrong

INFOMAX MATH READERS

Rosen Classroom™

New York

rh

Published in 2015 by The Rosen Publishing Group, Inc.
29 East 21st Street, New York, NY 10010

Book Design: Katelyn Londino

Photo Credits: Cover Design Pics/Thinkstock.com; p. 5 JPagetRFPhotos/Shutterstock.com; pp. 7, 9 Nordling/
Shutterstock.com; p. 11 (flags) Skazka Grez/Shutterstock.com; p. 11 (warning triangle) Corepics VOF/Shutterstock.com;
p. 13 cowardlion/Shutterstock.com; p. 15 slava17/Shutterstock.com; p. 17 (ice cubes) Suslik1983/Shutterstock.com;
p. 17 (boxes) andersphoto/Shutterstock.com; p. 17 (blocks) locrifa/Shutterstock.com; p. 19 Msgt. Ken Hammond/
Time & Life Pictures/Getty Images; p. 21 StudioSmart/Shutterstock.com; p. 22 Anton Petrus/Shutterstock.com.

ISBN: 978-1-4777-4737-7
6-pack ISBN: 978-1-4777-4735-3

Manufactured in the United States of America

CPSIA Compliance Information: Batch #WS15RC: For further information contact Rosen Publishing, New York, New York at 1-800-237-9932.

Contents

What Are Polygons?

Take a look at the objects around you. You may see windows, doors, and street signs. If you look more closely, you'll notice these objects are a lot like the shapes you learn about in math class.

Many objects are in the shape of circles, squares, triangles, and more. But only some of the shapes around us are polygons. Polygons are everywhere. Read on to find out where you can find them.

Polygons are flat shapes. Flat shapes lie in 1 **plane**, which is a flat surface. **Solid** shapes, such as cubes, are called **polyhedrons**.

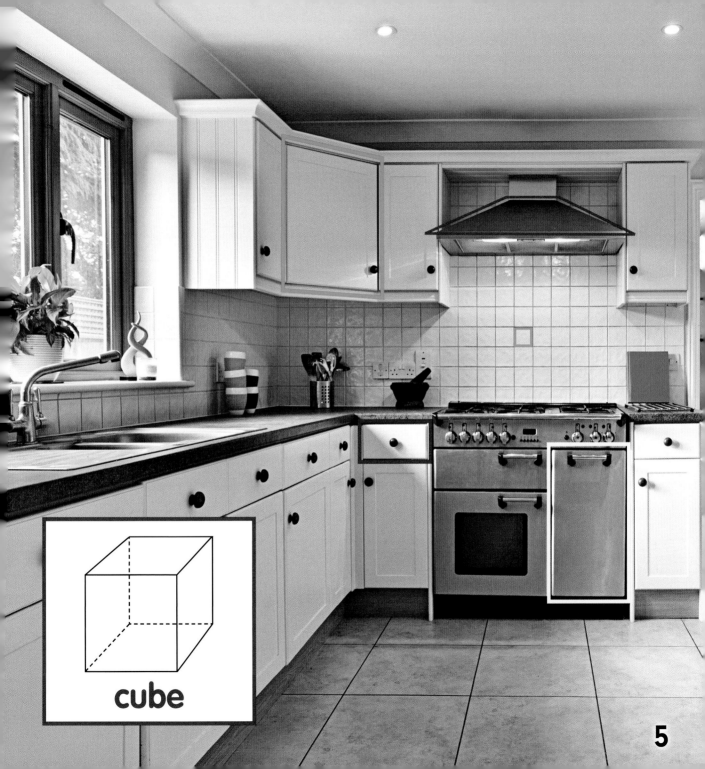

cube

Before you can **recognize** a polygon, you must know what it is. A shape is a polygon if it has at least 3 sides. It must also have at least 3 **angles**.

A polygon's sides must always be straight. If there are curves in a shape, it's not a polygon! Finally, polygons must always be closed. That means there are no openings, spaces, or breaks in its lines.

You can tell if a shape is closed if you can clearly see an area that's inside the shape and an area that's outside the shape.

Is it a polygon?

polygon	not a polygon

at least 3 sides

at least 3 angles

straight lines

closed shape

lies in 1 plane

7

Triangles Around Us

If you've ever seen a triangle, you've seen a polygon. A triangle is a flat shape with 3 straight sides. The sides touch each other with no spaces or openings, so it's a closed shape.

The places where the triangle's sides touch are very important. That's because those are the places where its angles are formed. A triangle has 3 angles, which is another reason why it's a polygon.

Triangles can have sides and angles that are different sizes. As long as there are 3 straight sides and 3 angles, it's a polygon.

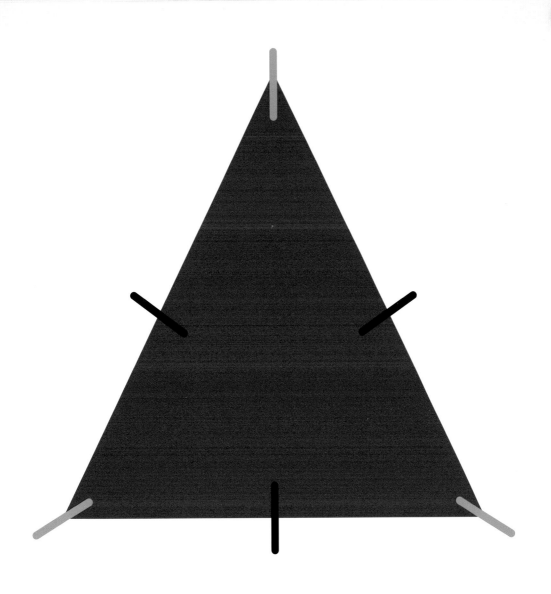

—— side **—— angle**

9

Sometimes we see triangles on the road. Drivers who need to pull over use road safety triangles. They let other drivers know there's a car or truck pulled over.

Where else can we spot triangles? Some flags have this shape. However, they don't look like road safety triangles. They're a different kind of triangle, but they're still polygons.

Where else can you find triangles?
Check your home or your classroom at school.
You're sure to find some there!

Quadrilaterals Are Everywhere

Shapes with 4 sides are also polygons, and we see them everywhere. Many windows are shaped like squares, and many doors are shaped like rectangles. Squares and rectangles both have 4 sides, which means they're **quadrilaterals**.

Quadrilaterals have 4 angles. Squares and rectangles have 4 equal angles, but some quadrilaterals have different-sized angles. Practice drawing quadrilaterals like the ones you see in this picture.

> Squares and rectangles are 2 kinds of quadrilaterals. A rhombus is a quadrilateral that looks like a slanted square. Trapezoids are quadrilaterals, too.

trapezoid

rhombus

square

rectangle

13

Quadrilaterals are one of the most common shapes because they include squares, rectangles, rhombuses, trapezoids, and more. Where in the world can you find these polygons? Look around you to find out.

Your desk at school has 4 sides. The folder you use for math class is a quadrilateral, too. All these objects are polygons. What are some other examples of quadrilaterals you see around you?

Are these shapes polygons?
How do you know?

What Is a Polyhedron?

Quadrilaterals can be put together to make a solid shape. When you put 6 squares together, you make a shape called a cube. A cube is a polyhedron because it's solid and lies in more than 1 plane. It has 6 faces and 8 corners.

Where can we find cubes? Look in your closet! Boxes are cubes that you use to store or move things from 1 place to another.

Polygons are flat shapes, while polyhedrons are solid shapes. These words share the prefix "poly," which means "many." That refers to their many sides and angles.

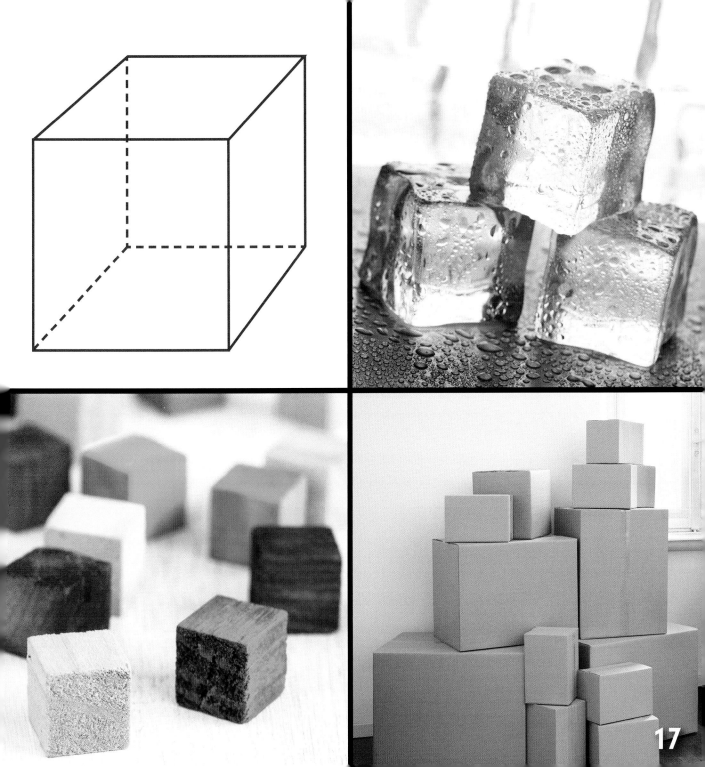

Shapes with Many Sides

Do you know what a pentagon is? A pentagon is a plane shape with 5 sides and 5 angles. It's a polygon because it has many sides and angles, its sides are straight, and it's a closed shape.

There's 1 pentagon that's very famous. It's a building in Washington, D.C., where our government works. It's called the Pentagon because that's the shape of the building!

Regular pentagons, such as this building, have equal sides and angles. **Irregular** pentagons have sides and angles of different sizes.

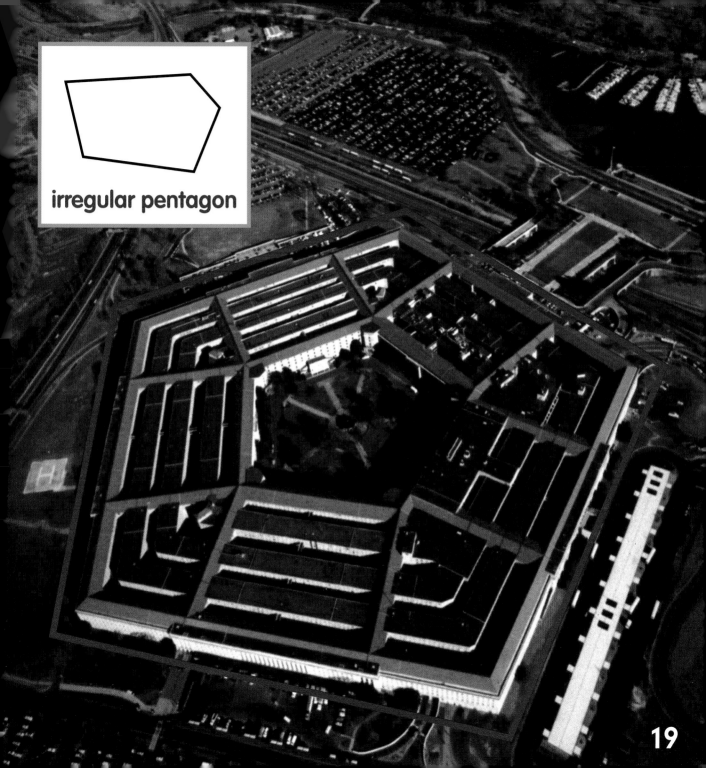

irregular pentagon

19

A 6-sided polygon is called a hexagon. A hexagon's 6 sides make 6 angles in the areas where they come together. Hexagons can have equal or unequal sides and angles, just like other polygons.

There's 1 animal that makes hexagons in their nest—honeybees. Honeybees make their honeycomb in the shape of hexagons. There can be thousands of hexagons in 1 bees' nest!

What other examples of hexagons can you see in the world around you?

Lots of Shapes

Polygons are everywhere, and they're easy to see if you're familiar with shapes. You can see flags that are triangles and windows that are squares. There are buildings shaped like pentagons. Road signs are shaped like many kinds of polygons. No matter where you go, you can find polygons.

Learning about polygons helps us understand objects in the world around us. Where else can you see polygons?

Glossary

angle (ANG-guhl) The space between two lines that cross or meet at the same point. Angles are measured in degrees.

irregular (ih-REH-gyuh-luhr) Not regular.

plane (PLAYN) A flat surface.

polyhedron (pah-lee-HEE-druhn) A solid shape with many faces.

quadrilateral (kwah-druh-LAA-tuh-ruhl) A figure with four sides.

recognize (REH-kihg-nyz) To know what something is because you've seen it before.

solid (SAH-luhd) A figure that takes up space.

Index